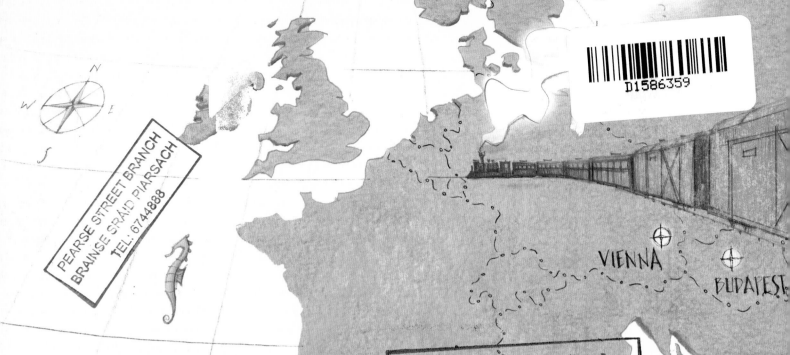

VIENNA

BUDAPEST

BARCELONA

HEDY'S JOURNEY

LISBON

The True Story of a Hungarian Girl
Fleeing the Holocaust

written by **Michelle Bisson**   *illustrated by* **El primo Ramón**

content consulting by **Narcisz Vida**
Educational Programme Specialist at Zachor Foundation, Hungary

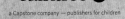

raintree
a Capstone company — publishers for children

Everyone always says how brave I was to travel through Europe on my own in the middle of World War II. I didn't think I was brave. I was Jewish, so I had no choice.

My cousin Marika was brave. The Nazis had already invaded Poland, where she was from. Ever since Hitler had taken power, my family was terrified. Hitler and his Nazis blamed the Jews for everything that was wrong in their country – and the world! We had heard about Hitler's concentration camps. Jews were being killed in them, so we feared for Marika's life.

Marika was staying with us in Budapest when the order came for all non-Hungarians to report to the deportation office. We offered to hide her – we begged her to stay. But she said no. She wanted to be with her parents and brother, no matter what happened.

When she got onto the train in September of 1941 she said, "I am only sorry I didn't get more out of life while I could." Marika understood that she was going to die.

I could not stop crying.

Even though we were Hungarian, we knew we were no longer safe in our own country. If the Nazis were coming for one Jew, it was only a matter of time before they came for us all.

The need to leave became even more urgent after the Nazi newspaper printed a story about my father, calling him the "king of the Jewish diamond jewellers". Nazis believed the Jews had stolen all the world's wealth. They were calling my father a thief!

When my little brother, Robert, went to get a copy of the newspaper, the newsagent patted him on the head. He called Robert a "good little Nazi". He had no idea Robert was Jewish. My brother held his tongue and turned away.

That summer the Hungarian Nazis had forced my 49-year-old father to spend three months in a labour camp as a "water boy". They let him out because of his service during World War I, in which Hungarians fought alongside Germans. But now it was different. Jews were considered the enemy. We knew that the next time he was taken to a camp, he might not come out alive.

Our Aunt Margaret in the United States helped us to fill in the paperwork needed to enter the US, where it was safer for Jews. Our visas came through, giving us permission to travel. We were going to leave! We had to get to Portugal to board a ship. But how to get there? Every train was packed, and every flight was booked. The only train we could find went through Germany. Worse, the travel agency could find only three tickets together. One of us would have to wait.

My brother was on my mother's passport, so they had to travel together. And we feared my father would be sent back to the labour camp if he stayed any longer.

That left only me.

I stayed with my favourite aunt, Cili, until it was my turn to leave a week and a half later.

"Be brave, Hedy," Cili said when she saw me off. "I'll be with you in spirit."

Her belief in me did give me strength. Because I didn't look Jewish, I made it through Austrian customs without being stopped. I tried hard to appear calm, but I couldn't stop sweating. I was in Nazi territory, alone. I prayed that I would get through it alive.

I chatted with a woman on the train. I tried not to think of all I was leaving behind. I pushed away thoughts of what might become of me if someone found out I was Jewish. I was terrified, but it was also an adventure. I had started to learn English at school, and I wanted to move to the United States. We thought of it as the land of opportunity. We'd had enough money to live comfortably in Hungary. But even before the war, Jews weren't treated well. We weren't even allowed to swim in the town pool. One night, my friend and I sneaked into the pool. We swam until our fingers turned to prunes!

When I got to Vienna, I was met by a young man called Kurt. The travel agent had asked him to look after me while I was there. Some people disagreed with Hitler and helped the Jews, and Kurt was one of them. He asked if he could escort me around town. I was nervous, but knew I'd feel even more scared if I sat alone in my hotel room. Besides, Kurt was young and handsome!

We took the cable car up to a beautiful spot lined with pine trees. The clean, fresh air felt wonderful to breathe after all that time trapped in fear on the train. The Nazis wouldn't be looking for me in this lovely place. Or so I thought.

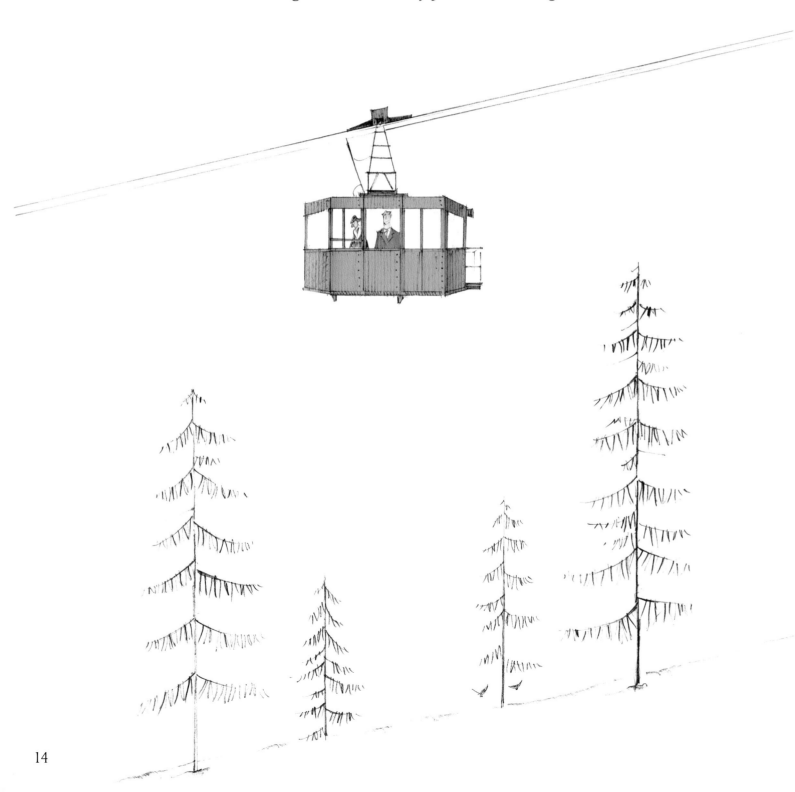

Then I saw them. A group of German soldiers standing on a patio. They were holding up beer mugs and belting out the Nazi Party anthem: "Clear the streets for the brown battalions! Clear the streets for the storm division!"

We were far enough away that no one could tell that Kurt and I were not singing along. Still, the peace of the place was now ruined for me. I was terrified the Nazis would realize I was Jewish and send me to a concentration camp. I wanted to be brave like Marika, but I wasn't. I couldn't stop trembling. "I need to go," I said to Kurt. "Please take me to my hotel."

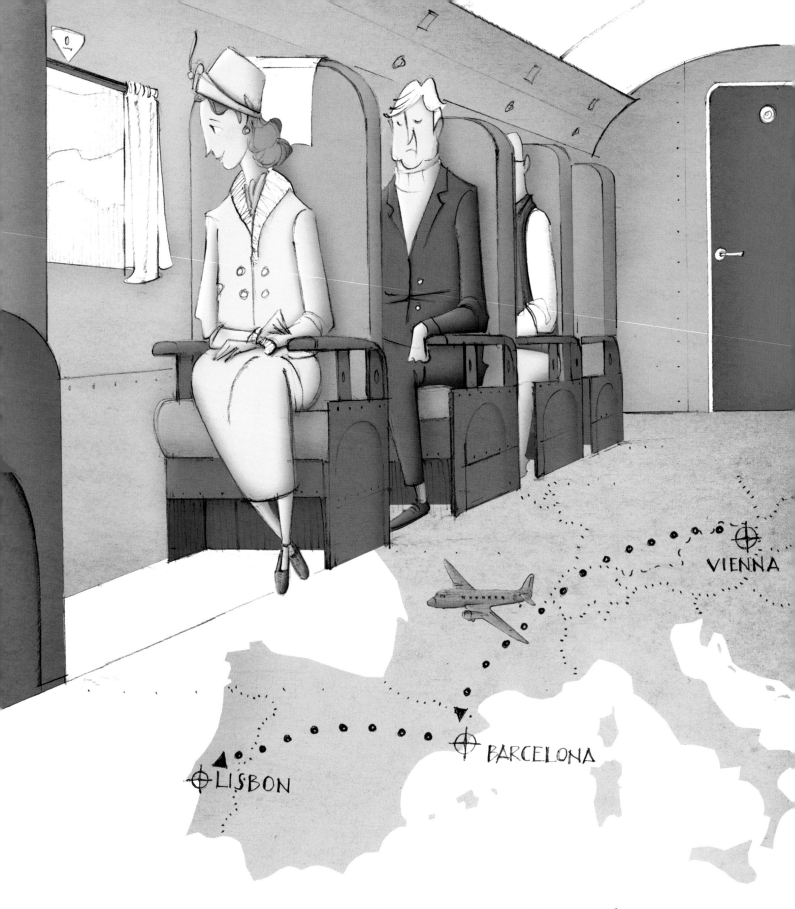

The flight to Barcelona was my first time on a plane, and I was excited to be in the air. But mostly I couldn't wait to be reunited with my parents and brother. My second flight would take me to them in Lisbon. When I saw my family, I couldn't stop crying. From happiness. And relief.

My father was not an affectionate man, but he hugged me, hard. That rare show of emotion only made me cry more. My mother and Robert each grabbed one of my hands. They wouldn't let go. We had all made it to a safe port in the storm of the Holocaust.

In a week it would be time to board the ship to the United States.

"Extra! Extra!" newsboys shouted as we walked along the seashore.

It was 7 December 1941 — the day of Japan's horrible attack on Pearl Harbor, a US Navy base in Hawaii. The United States entered the war. The ship we had planned to take the following week was no longer available. There would be no more US passenger ships going to New York. The tickets we had bought were now worthless.

GUERRA!

O JAPÃO ATACA PEARL HARBOR

We discovered that a Portuguese boat would be taking about 500 refugees to South America and Cuba. It would also take 100 refugees to New York – those who, like my family, had been lucky enough to get visas to enter the United States. Everyone on the boat needed a new home. Like us, they were fleeing for religious or political reasons.

We gave some of the jewellery we had smuggled out of Hungary to one of the officials and his wife. She promised us places on the boat.

We couldn't stop smiling as we walked to the travel agency to collect the tickets we'd been promised. But our hearts broke when they told us there were no tickets for us after all. The bribe had not been enough. They wanted more money.

This was the turning point of our lives. Should we stay and keep trying, or should we go back to Budapest? Either way, we would need money. Ours was quickly running out.

My father wanted to go back to Hungary. My mother and I said no. The Hungarian Nazis had segregated all the schools and fired many Jewish workers. When Jews left, non-Jews stole their belongings and often moved into their homes. We might have nothing at all to go home to, even if we could get back. My mother and I believed the United States was our only hope.

Once again, we got lucky.

My father's brother Willie, who now lived in Chile, was able to send us the fare we needed to board the ship.

On 28 January 1942, two long months after we had arrived in Lisbon, we finally departed. We were to sail to Cuba and Chile, and then to our port of call – New York.

But things didn't go according to plan.

First, the ship stopped in Casablanca to pick up 500 more refugees. More than 1,000 passengers were now squeezed onto a ship meant for half that number.

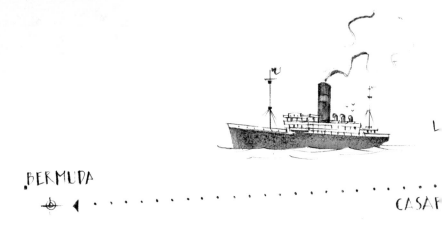

BERMUDA

CASA

I was horribly seasick. I could barely eat. The queues for the bathroom were so long that it was hard to get clean. But that wasn't the worst of it. Our ship ran on coal and, after a few weeks, the coal supplies were running out. We would not have enough to get to Cuba.

We stopped in Bermuda, but Bermuda had no coal to spare. We couldn't get off the boat, but we enjoyed sailing around the island. The peaceful little towns and people pedalling on bicycles were lovely to watch after so much time at sea. But then something unimaginable happened.

An adorable two-year-old boy on the ship had brightened our days. His joy had helped us to forget our troubles. One day he was playing peek-a-boo with friends, and he fell through an open hatch into the ship's engine room.

The fall killed him instantly.

I was sad and shocked and haunted. Not since Marika's deportation had I been so aware of the reality of the war. This young boy had escaped the Nazis. But it was still the war — having to flee his own home — that caused his death.

Now, more desperately than ever, we wanted to make it to safety in the United States.

In the end, Bermuda provided just enough coal to get us to the United States. We got as far as Newport News, Virginia. The 900 passengers with visas for other countries couldn't set foot on US shores. The rest of us had to stay on the ship too, while we waited for more coal so we could continue our journey.

We couldn't bear the idea of waiting any longer on that crowded ship. Not when we were so close to our new home.

Those of us on board who had visas to enter the United States sent a telegram to President Franklin D. Roosevelt. We asked to be allowed off the boat in Virginia instead of New York.

He agreed! As long as we could pay our train fare to Pennsylvania Station in New York City. With the help of the Jewish charity HIAS, we all could.

We had landed on US shores on 22 February 1942. It was George Washington's birthday. The United States was our home now.

We had escaped the Nazis. And we were free.

NEW YORK

NEWPORT NEWS

BERMUDA

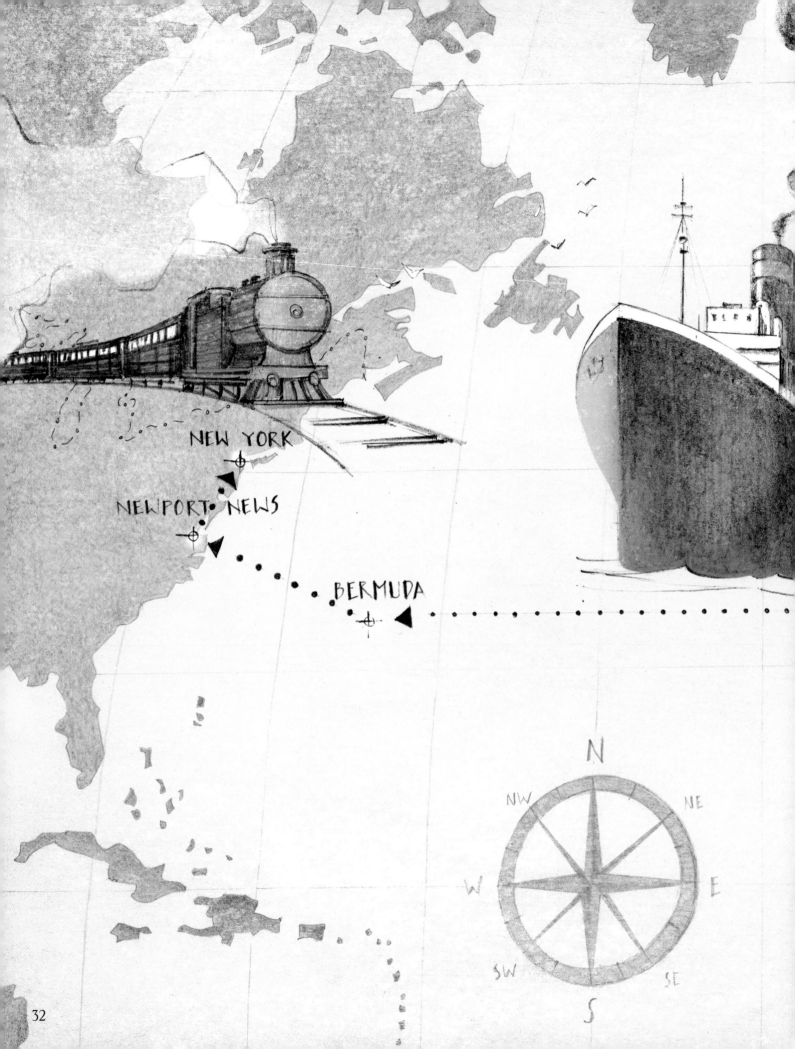

NEW YORK

NEWPORT NEWS

BERMUDA

N
NW   NE
W   E
SW   SE
S

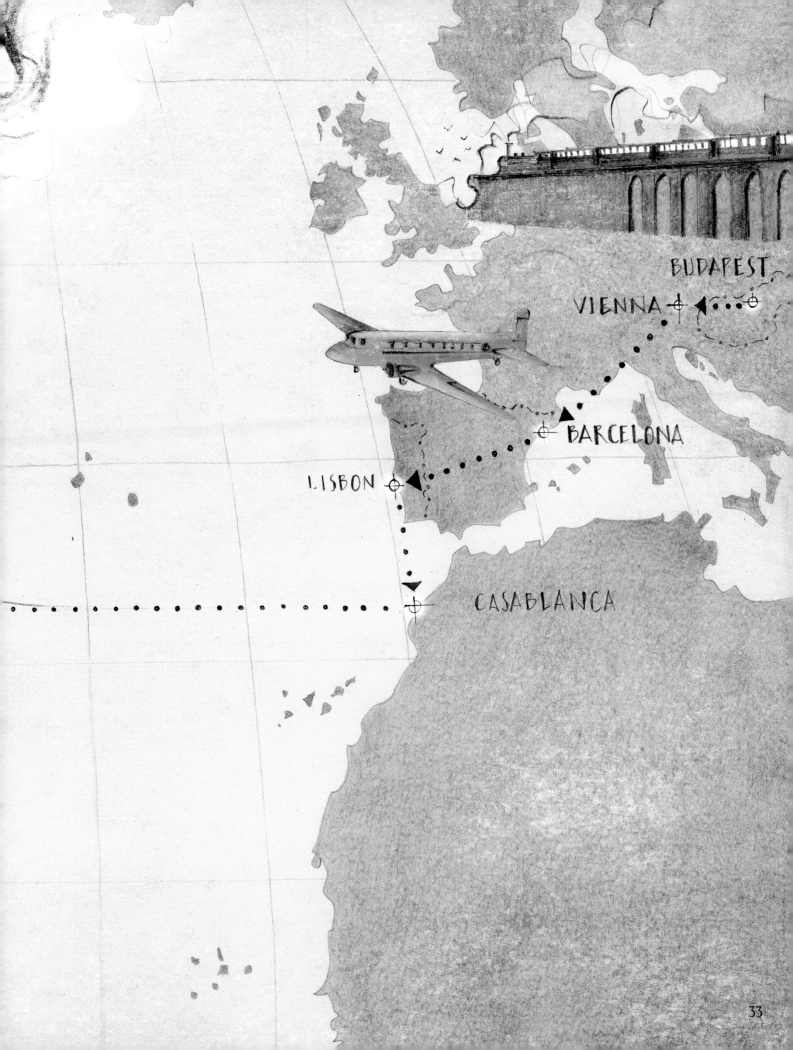

BUDAPEST

VIENNA

BARCELONA

LISBON

CASABLANCA

TIMELINE

January 1933
Adolf Hitler is appointed chancellor of Germany and soon begins sending people who oppose his Nazi party to concentration camps.

1938–1939
Germany begins to occupy neighbouring countries.

September 1939
Germany invades Poland. As a result, France and Great Britain declare war on Germany. Great Britain and France are known as "the Allies". Other countries slowly join in.

September 1940
Germany, Japan and Italy sign the Tripartite Pact. They are known as "the Axis".

Summer 1941
Hedy's father is imprisoned in a labour camp. Marika is deported.

September 1941
Hedy and her family decide to leave Hungary.

7 December 1941
The bombing of Pearl Harbor in Hawaii by Japan leaves Hedy and her family stranded in Portugal without a ship to take them to the United States.

8 December 1941
The United States enters World War II on the side of the Allies.

28 January 1942
Hedy and her family finally set sail on a ship called *Nyassa*. Hedy is 16.

Winter 1942
The *Nyassa* makes stops in Casablanca and Bermuda.

22 February 1942
Hedy and her family reach the United States.

15 May 1944
Hungarian Jews are deported to gas chambers at Auschwitz concentration camp. One half of all Jews killed at Auschwitz were Hungarian.

27 January 1945
Russian troops liberate Auschwitz.

7 May 1945
Germany surrenders to the Allies.

August 1945
The United States drops two atomic bombs on Japan, the first on Hiroshima and the second on Nagasaki.

2 September 1945
Japan surrenders to the United States, ending the war. Unknown to Hedy at the time, September 2 was also her future husband's birthday.

Hedy and her mother in Hungary

Hedy's Hungarian passport photo

THE REST OF HEDY'S STORY

Hedy and her family were thrilled to be in the United States. The Red Cross volunteers were kind to them. They brought them sandwiches to eat on the train. Hedy's family had never seen white bread before. They thought it was cardboard and threw it away! But they discovered that the meat was delicious. There was much they'd need to learn about their new home.

Hedy and her parents didn't have much money, and they had to learn new ways. They learned English. They got jobs. They rebuilt their lives. They did experience anti-Semitism and discrimination against immigrants, but they did not fear for their lives.

Hedy married an American whom she met on the way home from night school. His mother wasn't thrilled that her son was marrying an immigrant, but he prevailed. They had three children who each, in their way, grew up to personify the American dream: a lawyer, a business owner and a writer — me. Hedy was my mother, and I am the girl in the illustration on page 3 and in the photographs on page 36.

It wasn't until I was 12 years old that I learned there had even been a Holocaust. My teacher at school told us about the terrible concentration camps the Nazis had built during World War II and the horrific things they did to people there. I couldn't believe it. I went home and asked my mother if it was true.

"Yes," she said. And that was why they had to flee.

Slowly, over the years, I learned the rest of my mother's story.

She told me that when she and her parents boarded the train for New York, the first thing they saw were signs reading "Whites Only" and "Colored Only". They were stunned. My mother vowed then to help the less fortunate and to fight against inequality. That was a lesson she taught me.

I also learned that the "M" in my name was a tribute to my brave cousin Marika. I learned that my mother honoured her this way not because Marika died, but because she had courage. And I learned that my mother was braver than she knew, braver than she understood at the time.

My mother is gone now, as are her parents and her brother, Robert. Those of us still alive mourn both those who survived the Holocaust, like my mother and her family, as well as those who were killed by the Nazis, including:

> my cousin Marika
>
> my uncle Laci
>
> my uncle Jozsi

… and the more than 500,000 other Hungarian Jews killed when the Germans invaded in the last year of the war.

Six million Jews were killed by the Nazis in Europe altogether. Eleven million people were exterminated overall, including gay people, disabled people, political opponents and others the Nazis considered less than human.

The survivors, their children, grandchildren and great-grandchildren remember, honour, and tell their stories.

Michelle and her brothers, Darryl (left) and Larry, in Atlantic City, New Jersey

Hedy, Michelle and Robert celebrating Hedy's 80th birthday

Hedy, 1945, aged 20

Hedy and Rus on their engagement day

Hedy's mother and father and her brother, Robert, in Red Bank, New Jersey

Hedy's Aunt Margaret, who helped her family get to the US

GLOSSARY

anti-Semitism discrimination against Jewish people

concentration camp prison camp where masses of people, such as prisoners of war, political prisoners or refugees, are held under harsh conditions

deportation forcing people to go back to their country of origin

HIAS charitable organization founded in 1881 to assist Jews fleeing persecution and which now also assists non-Jewish refugees

Holocaust during World War II, the mass murder of six million Jews, as well as political and religious leaders, and Romani, disabled and homosexual people

Nazi member of a political party led by Adolf Hitler; the Nazis ruled Germany from 1933 to 1945

prejudice hatred or unfair treatment of people who belong to a certain group such as a race or religion

refugee person forced to flee his or her home because of natural disaster, war or persecution

telegram message sent by telegraph, which is a machine that uses electrical signals to send messages over long distances

visa government document giving a person permission to enter a foreign country

FURTHER READING

Jars of Hope: How One Woman Helped Save 2,500 Children During the Holocaust, Jennifer Roy (Raintree, 2015)

Saving the Persecuted (Heroes of World War II), Brenda and Brian Williams (Raintree, 2015)

Survivors of the Holocaust, Kath Shackleton (Franklin Watts, 2016)

WEBSITES

www.bbc.co.uk/newsround/16690175
What was the Holocaust?

www.bbc.co.uk/programmes/p0274903
Watch an animation of Ruth and her family's escape from Nazi Germany.

www.dkfindout.com/uk/history/world-war-ii/
Find out more about the people and events of World War II.

ABOUT THE AUTHOR

Michelle Bisson is an award-winning journalist and playwright who has worked as a children's book editor for more decades than she cares to share. Hedy's Journey is her first picture book. It is based on her mother's written memories of her journey to the United States during the Holocaust, as well as the many stories she told of her life in Hungary. Hedy died several years ago, but this book will help her live on. Michelle lives just outside of New York City in Tarrytown, New York, USA.

ABOUT THE ILLUSTRATOR

Borja Ramón López Cotelo, also known as el primo Ramón, is a PhD architect who started working as an illustrator for Spanish architectural magazines shortly after he began his career. Together with Maria Olmo, his partner, he has made illustrated works for international publishing houses (Usborne Publishing, Pearson ELT, Oxford University Press) and communication agencies (VCCP London). They are also authors and illustrators of *Las cosas que importan* (ed. Bululú), launched in Spain in 2015, and to be published in China in 2017.

Raintree is an imprint of Capstone Global Library Limited, a company incorporated in England and Wales having its registered office at 264 Banbury Road, Oxford, OX2 7DY – Registered company number: 6695582

www.raintree.co.uk
myorders@raintree.co.uk

Text © Capstone Global Library Limited 2017
The moral rights of the proprietor have been asserted.

Edited by Kristen Mohn
Designed by Ashlee Suker
Illustrated by el primo Ramón
Original illustrations © Capstone Global Library Limited 2017
Picture research by Tracy Cummins
Production by Tori Abraham
Originated by Capstone Global Library Limited
Printed and bound in China

ISBN 978-1-4747-4300-6
21 20 19 18 17
10 9 8 7 6 5 4 3 2 1

British Library Cataloguing in Publication Data
A full catalogue record for this book is available from the British Library.

Acknowledgements
We would like to thank the following for permission to reproduce photographs: Michelle Bisson, pages 35, 36, 37
We would like to thank Narcisz Vida, Educational Programme Specialist at Zachor Foundation, Hungary, for his invaluable help in the preparation of this book.

Every effort has been made to contact copyright holders of material reproduced in this book. Any omissions will be rectified in subsequent printings if notice is given to the publisher.

All the Internet addresses (URLs) given in this book were valid at the time of going to press. However, due to the dynamic nature of the Internet, some addresses may have changed, or sites may have changed or ceased to exist since publication. While the author and publisher regret any inconvenience this may cause readers, no responsibility for any such changes can be accepted by either the author or the publisher.